W9-CFA-256

DIGITAL AND INFORMATION LITERACY ™

RESEARCH PROJECT SUCCESS USING DIGITAL TOOLS

PETE MICHALSKI AND HENRIETTA M. LILY

rosen publishing's
rosen
central®

New York

Published in 2016 by The Rosen Publishing Group, Inc.
29 East 21st Street, New York, NY 10010

Library of Congress Cataloging-in-Publication Data

Names: Michalski, Pete, author. | Lily, Henrietta M., author.
Title: Research project success using digital tools / Pete Michalski and Henrietta Lily.
Description: First edition. | New York, NY : The Rosen Publishing Group, Inc., 2016. | Series: Digital and information literacy | Includes bibliographical references.
Identifiers: LCCN 2015033391 | ISBN 978-1-4994-3787-4 (library bound) — 978-1-4994-3785-0 (paperback) — 978-1-4994-3786-7 (6-pack)
Subjects: LCSH: Internet research–Juvenile literature. | Electronic information resource searching–Juvenile literature. | Research–Methodology–Juvenile literature. |
Classification: LCC ZA4228 .C437 2016 | DDC 001.4/202854678–dc23
LC record available at http://lccn.loc.gov/2015033391

Manufactured in the United States of America

CONTENTS

INTRODUCTION

Throughout their academic careers, students write essays, book reports, and create many other written projects and presentations. After graduation, even beyond college and graduate school, many must keep their communication and writing skills sharp. Many projects require that writers and researchers get up to speed on subjects quickly.

If a topic is truly relevant, or at least interesting, to the public, many sources, such as newspapers and websites, will offer content related to it. The ease and speed of online publishing means that many versions of the same content can circulate within seconds, minutes, and hours. Online sources compete against each other to offer all there is to know on a topic. Sometimes, this means that rival sources and information platforms may sacrifice hard, proven facts for unproven ones, or ones that are just plain wrong.

Every topic comes with a body of knowledge that is considered established or factual. One definition of a fact is something that can be proven or is indisputably true and can be used as evidence for a larger case or position. For example, that President Barack Obama is a member of the Democratic Party is a fact.

There are also many bits of data or content online that are not necessarily facts. Unproven assertions might be preceded by a phrase like, "It has

A good teacher will create a challenging but fair assignment for you to sharpen your research skills and will provide guidance on how to achieve your goals by using the Internet and electronic databases to find sources of all kinds.

been reported that . . ." In other words, someone claimed a thing to be the case at some time. A piece of information was disclosed and was believable enough to repeat or consider but has not been proven, or substantiated.

Doing a report based on facts means researching these details and determining which are fact or fiction. The quickest way to do that is to evaluate all of the sources and trim the fat.

Some sources are more believable and legitmate than others. On the other end of the spectrum are sources that a serious researcher should never cite. Writers needs to be savvy enough to separate trusted sources from untrustworthy ones. Authorities on a topic, or professionals in a field, are often trusted sources, though even they may bend the truth or misinform at times. However, you can generally rely on hard data and information provided by governments, universities, foundations, museums, and similar sources. Their online presence will hopefully have the most current information available. A company or individual may also be trusted to provide factual content, as long it can be substantiated by other sources. When possible, it always makes a researcher's case strongest when he or she cites from an original source.

Content or assertions that cannot be traced back to a trustworthy source, and cannot be substantiated, should not be trusted. At the very least, they should not be used to support a position in a persuasive essay nor augment the findings of a report or presentation. This book can be used to help writers and researchers navigate the sometimes overwhelming online landscape, helping them become cybersleuths equipped to collect information on people, places, and events and allowing them to write on many different types of topics.

Chapter 1

Starting Online Research

The vast, worldwide system of computer networks connected together known as the Internet, along with the World Wide Web that rides atop that Internet and gives us the means with which to access the Internet, has changed forever how we do research. Web pages from the simplest personal blog to massive social media platforms like Facebook all contribute. Google chief executive officer (CEO) Eric Schmidt has been quoted as saying that the Internet now has at least 5 million terabytes of data (each terabyte equals 1,000 gigabytes), adding that Google itself, the world's largest indexer of data, has perhaps indexed only 0.004% of the total size.

These enormous resources are made available through one's browser, an application, or a program that gives one's computer instructions to carry out tasks. The user interacts with the many collections of content available online, including text, images, movies, and interactive data. The surfer simply types the address of the desired website in the browser's address field and hits return. Almost instantly, the surfer will be looking at the welcome

These days, doing thorough research can mean not even having to make it to an actual library, though library resources remain valuable. Anyone with an Internet connection has access to a world of knowledge.

page of the site he or she wanted to visit in the browser window. Or he or she merely needs to enter a search term on a search engine, like Google or Yahoo! Search, and a list of hits best matching his or her request will appear.

Browsing Away: Choose Your Weapon

Not all browsers are created equal, even if many share all of the same basic characteristics. Great researchers get to know a few different browsers because each has features that are exclusive to that browser. Common browsers include Safari, Google Chrome, Mozilla Firefox, Opera, Internet Explorer, and many others.

Web pages are made with HTML (hypertext markup language) and other types of code that determine what the users will see and experience. Coding creates neat features like background color, animations, and buttons. Each browser interprets the programming of each website to reproduce it, but it isn't always the same across browsers. Some content may not work with outdated browsers, and websites may automatically report that you, the researcher, should upgrade to a newer version of your browser.

The wrong browser can also cause problems when requesting information. When filling out online forms or requests, researchers may find that they can't complete the process. Maybe they get to a certain stage and then an error message loads, or they are booted from the system. Trying another browser may result in the same process occurring smoothly. With any website, if a feature isn't loading or happening properly, the researcher should always try another browser before giving up.

For home use, there are many free browsers that can be downloaded. Some sites may ask researchers to upgrade the current browser in order to see newer features. If the computer being used is not the researcher's own, he or she needs to ask permission from the owner or school before downloading any new applications or upgrades. Most computers at a high school or university will have several browsers installed.

Proprietary Browsers and Networks

Certain electronic resources, such as digital library collections, may have custom-built browsers. The information is kept on a private network, and in some cases this information isn't accessible through the Web. If the local library has electronic collections on a private network, the savvy researcher will take some time to get to know the browser.

Libraries offer classes and tutorials to learn how to best use custom-made applications. Such classes will likely provide you with some neat research tricks. The browser is a powerful tool, but it can't tell the researcher where to go. Think of the browser as a doorway through which you, the researcher, must walk. Once you are on the other side, your direction is all up to you.

Bots, Crawlers, and Spiders (Oh, My!)

The Internet is organized into millions of web portals. There are also inactive sites. It would be impossible to know what all of these sites were without some sort of organizational framework. Without indexing and other ways of organizing search data, researchers would truly be at a loss to find much of anything, unless they knew ahead of time exactly what they were looking for. Often, that is not the case.

Although researching once required hours of legwork, the search bar in web browsers has allowed us to streamline the quest for relevant articles, reports, and other content.

A search engine is a tool that searches the Web for information. The system uses web robots, which are also known as bots, crawlers, and spiders. Bots are applications that run automatically. The bots crawl through the Web, updating links and copying what they find. Search engines index or put this information into categories. When the surfer is ready to find something about a topic, dozens of bots have already crawled through old and new sites.

Dozens of search engines have indexed this information. They're just waiting for the researcher to come look. Popular search engines include Google, Yahoo! Search, and Bing. When the researcher visits these search sites and enters a keyword or name, the search engine returns tens, hundreds, or thousands of Web addresses. There are also metasearch engines. Metasearch engines search the search engines themselves. They return the top-ranking results from many search engines. By using a metasearch engine, the researcher is accessing several search engines at once. Metasearch engines include Excite, HotBot, info.com, and Dogpile.

Although metasearch engines look at many search engines, they are computer-based and automatic. Each metasearch engine follows its own instructions to retrieve information from other search engines. Some search for the most common results. This means that the researcher isn't getting a deep dive into each search engine but is just skimming what's popular. When using metasearch engines, it's best to use at least two for truly thorough research. Then compare what each one finds. For the best results, a researcher should make sure to search with keywords that are unique to the topic. The searcher should scroll through more than one listing of results to make sure that he or she has reached far and wide enough.

What Do You Want to Find Out?

A good rule of thumb is to always follow the instructions that the teacher or instructor provides for each project. The teacher may require that the researcher present notes along with the final report. It's always best to ask for examples of what is expected in notes and supporting materials. These are often detailed in the assignment itself, or may be covered during another lesson.

The next step is to create a list of questions about the topic that will be answered through the research. A summary or outline can emerge from the questions. Once the list, summary, or outline is made, research can begin. However you collect the results of your online research (whatever types of content they may be), you should keep them in one handy place, whether it's a folder on your desktop, on a hard drive or flash drive, or, nowadays, uploaded on a remote server somewhere ("in the cloud," for example).

Different researchers have different styles. Some like to read online and select only a few facts and websites in their notes. Some like to gather many

A USB flash drive or similar kind of detachable storage device is an important tool if you are doing research away from home. It is also useful to have a backup device with all your files if your computer breaks down or is infected with a virus.

sites and facts at once and then read through them while offline. Whatever the case, the researcher needs to copy the URL of each and every website used for gathering facts. The section or contents of the page need to be linked to the website in supporting documents.

Atop every bit of info or passage that is cut and pasted, the researcher should label it with the source—for instance, "Mayo Clinic, Topic: Acne." He or she should copy and paste the URL of the content and organize it so it is easy to find and reference (and cite) later. It's also important to type in the date the material was found on the Web, and sometimes even the time, depending on the research. Websites can change overnight.

To organize large amounts of collected content, highlight or underline the facts that support the topic or position. After the research is completed, it will be easy for the researcher to scroll through the document and find the facts that he or she thinks are worth using. All of the facts need to have the original source mentioned along with them, so keeping organized like this will save time.

If cutting and pasting highlighted facts into a rough outline or first draft essay, the researcher must cut and paste the link or source along with it. During the writing stage, the researcher might find that he or she needs a little more insight in relation to a found fact. Having the original source along with it will allow the researcher to quickly go back to the link or links. He or she will be able to reread the research and gain further support for the point of view. Anything that is copied and pasted from another source must have the source information along with it.

Narrowing It Down

The results of one's research can sometimes even hinder one's work. If the researcher does too broad a sweep of a subject, he or she will get thousands of results. Weeding through the results will take a lot of time. If the researcher does a specific sweep, he or she might miss some interesting details found outside of what is being researched. Finding a balance through organized researching is key.

The researcher should begin the research process by creating a brief summary or outline. When given a topic, the researcher should take a moment to think about it before diving right into the Web. He or she should consider what is being asked. Is the researcher being asked to explain the details about a person, place, or event in a straightforward manner? This is a descriptive essay. The researcher should search for broadly known facts about the topic. Is the project to evaluate a person's life, a place, or event,

If you have any confusion about an assignment, talking it over with classmates or friends might help clear it up. A fellow student might need help figuring out the aims of his or her own project, too.

and give an opinion? This is a persuasive essay. The researcher should search for any facts that support the point of view. Is the project for comparing two concepts, highlighting similarities or differences? This is a comparative essay. The researcher will need to dig into both topics.

Determine what kind of research you are doing—what questions are being asked, or what are their aims—and you can then put the research aim into words, preferably in the form of a short paragraph. What is being written, and what will you share with the reader? Furthermore, the researcher should contemplate other topics or keywords closely related to the one at hand. This enriches the main topic, gives the researcher a larger context, and can also help the researcher establish boundaries. What lies outside the topic helps define the topic itself, in other words.

Chapter 2

Exploring Primary Sources

Primary sources are documents or things that were written or created during the time being researched. These may be original documents, such as speeches, manuscripts, letters, or diaries; official records such as birth certificates; or other documentation. They may also be creative works, like books and artwork; relics and artifacts, such as engravings, furniture, clothing; or audiovisual records like television footage or radio recordings.

For a topic that overlaps with the modern era, primary sources record important developments up through the present, including ongoing activity. Using the example of the volcano eruption at Krakatoa, primary sources include documents and illustrations from the time of its eruption in 1883. Letters, lithographs, maps, and any correspondence of those reporting the eruption are also primary sources. Today, access to the volcano is restricted to scientists and emergency personnel. Any scientific correspondence, maps, graphs, images, and artifacts from these people are also primary sources. Every time an eruption or event occurs, the supporting documents and artifacts become related primary sources.

File　Edit　View　Favorites　Tools　Help

HIDDEN AGENDAS AND THE "OFFICIAL STORY

Hidden Agendas and the "Official Story"

Even if accessing a site with lots of primary source information, the savvy researcher must be careful. Some foundations and organizations are formed to promote a certain idea to the public. They may not offer the complete story. They may offer materials that create a version of the truth, but not the whole truth. The smart researcher approaches a site as if it must prove itself as valid before its facts can pass the test. The "official story" on a foundation's website, and even on a government site of a municipality, state, or the federal government, might be promoting a hidden agenda. When in doubt, always compare the official account with other sources. This is especially true when it comes to topics such as sociology, history, and other subjective fields.

Researchers and writers should always try to use at least one primary source. Primary sources often provide information that isn't repeated all across the Web. By digging deep, the researcher might be able to provide interesting information that his or her audience—and even his or her teacher—may have not heard before. If the essay is able to reveal something new, it goes from being an average essay to being a success.

Primary Sources in the Digital Era

In a big city, a researcher might be lucky enough to have access to a library, even a research or university library. Many of these libraries will have authentic primary sources in special collections. A patron might need special permission to see these documents and artifacts. To make these rare historic items available to all of us, libraries rely upon computers. Many primary source items are digitized, copied, scanned, or photographed. The files are converted to electronic formats like PDFs and JPEGs.

This process of converting paper-based and other content into electronic data is known as digitization. Digitization can make these documents accessible to anyone with an Internet connection, even half a world away. Electronic and digital collections allow students to take an up-close look at documents they may never get to see in real life, such as the actual U.S. Constitution.

Digital assets have democratized research for those who cannot dedicate the time or the money for reproductions of primary sources, such as this old illustration of the volcanic island of Krakatoa from Theodore Alexander Weber.

If you are prevented from accessing a digital collection or database, call or send an e-mail to the library, explaining that you are a student working on an essay. Be sure to include the topic in your e-mail. A librarian or other staff member will likely be able to walk you through accessing the digital library. If it's a truly private collection, or restricted to certain members of a profession, the librarian representative may provide other alternatives.

Students can also speak to their own school librarians about the resources they're trying to access. They may be able to locate the desired electronic files or provide alternatives.

To search for collections containing information about a historic person, for example, a researcher can use a search engine. The researcher would enter the name and the word "library," "collection," or "exhibit." This will usually yield a few library-based websites about the person or related persons.

Any interviews with the subject or with key figures related to the subject are also considered primary sources. Most interviews are published in newspapers, journals, magazines, or books. LexisNexis, the

Here is the main reading room of the U.S. Library of Congress, another institution that has digitized many assets for public, remote access.

well-known, searchable database for legal cases and news articles, offers a specific portal for accessing such information through the Web. It connects users to private sources, collections, news sources, journals, and magazines. Researchers can specify a range of dates from which they'd like to see articles or cases. The service is far-reaching and thorough, pulling up articles from every major and minor publication.

SEPTEMBER 29, 1883. HARPER'S WEEKLY. 613

THE ISLAND AND VOLCANO OF KRAKATOA, STRAIT OF SUNDA, SUBMERGED DURING THE LATE ERUPTION.—[See Page 614.]

Reproductions or representations of primary sources that are physical objects have also proliferated in digital collections. This image of an original 1883 wood engraving could help augment a presentation on the Krakatoan eruption.

Pick a Topic, Any Topic

There are many different databases, covering every major subject conceivable. Libraries usually subscribe to different databases, especially if their own collections are not extensive. Subject-based databases include WHOLIS (the World Health Organization Library Database), for health and medicine, and Anthropology Plus, for news, articles, journals, and full texts relating to anthropology. TRIS is a database from the U.S. Department of Transportation. It has over half a million records about research in the field of transportation. Oxford Art Online contains more than forty-five thousand articles about art.

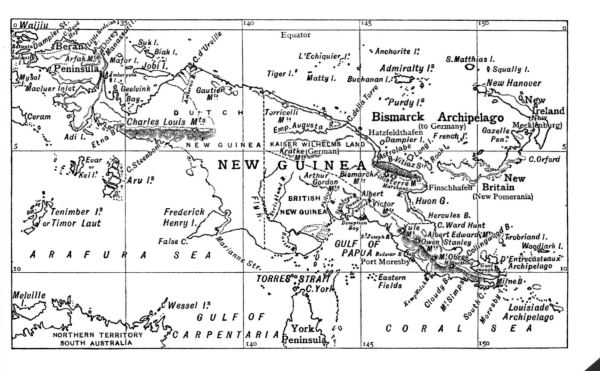

Digitized assets also help protect original, fragile sources, such as this antique map of New Guinea, many of which can be damaged by handling or even by photographing them excessively.

Consider some of the historical topics you may research during your school career: the history of African Americans and civil rights, women's suffrage, and the history of the presidency, among many others. Databases accessible to you in your own local library and school are likely to give you all you need to perform thorough research. Historical maps, documents, illustrations, and other sources you may be barred from handling in person are reproduced in detail and viewable via these databases. All you will need is a username and password provided to you by a librarian or other staffer. If you cannot find what you need at your own library, your main local branch might be a better bet.

MYTHS & FACTS

MYTH Any government website can be trusted as completely reliable.

FACT Even governments—whether those of the United States or your state, city, or town—can post biased or incorrect information. With foreign governments, those who are rivals or enemies can publish conflicting information. Thus, it is advisable to review information from both sides and from impartial observers.

MYTH Good reliable information costs money.

FACT Most information about a common topic is available for free somewhere in the world. Avoid paying for any information before doing a thorough search for it. The type of essays in school will be on topics where information is readily available and free.

MYTH The newest information is always online.

FACT Not all information is up to date on the Internet, even at government and academic sites. If the topic relies on the latest information, the researcher must make sure that the information is current.

Chapter 3

Exploring Secondary Sources

One step removed from primary sources are secondary sources. Primary sources may often be the basis for these secondary sources. The latter include journal, newspaper, and magazine articles; books; essays; reports; and studies that quote or reference information or events related to the primary sources. Some of these sources are produced with the intent of tying up or interpreting a thing or event. They provide further insight and context, hopefully relying on known facts.

Sometimes a third type of source compiles primary and secondary sources. Called tertiary sources, these are where primary and secondary resources are collected in one place. The third source includes manuals, textbooks, fact books, almanacs, encyclopedias, and guidebooks.

An overview of all three types of sources can be made using the example of the civil rights leader Martin Luther King Jr. There are letters he wrote, which are primary sources. The Nobel Foundation, which awards the Nobel Prize, has a web page on him. This is a secondary source. It may even include the texts of his letters and speeches. There are also biographies of

One of the most common examples of a tertiary source is an encyclopedia, such as the well-known one published for years by Britannica. It is trusted in large part because the information within has been carefully vetted.

King, which also are secondary sources. If someone else wants to create an encyclopedia of the civil rights movement, the publisher will use passages from his letters and even include information obtained from the Nobel Foundation website. All of these sources are pulled together in the tertiary source—for example, the encyclopedia, or an American history textbook.

Evaluate, Confirm, and Verify

Commercial or business websites make claims that must be scrutinized more closely. Most information about the owner of a website can be found by navigating to the "About" section or "History" section if there is one. Poking around the website will provide clues as to a company's stance on issues, whether it is biased or impartial about certain facts, and many other criteria to evaluate its trustworthiness.

Even a site whose owners have a particular agenda can provide good information and even reliable facts and data. Researchers still need to ensure that these can be fact-checked elsewhere—for example, on a government, educational, museum, or foundation site, or even a reputable news or academic periodical. Commercial sites can easily be distinguished from governmental or nonprofit websites. For example:

.com: A commercial or company site; sometimes an individual's site
.net: A commercial/company site or individual's site
.gov: A site funded or operated by the government
.edu: An academic site, such as a university library or collection
.org: A site for an organization, foundation, or museum; can also be an individual's site

There aren't strict laws that make an individual or company stick to a particular address. At the very least, .gov and .edu sites are more reliably impartial. They are relatively trustworthy because creating, posting, and modifying content on these sites is done only by government or academic professionals, who are more accountable for the veracity of their content, usually, than corporations or other private entities, such as individuals.

Let's take the example of a researcher studying STDs among teens. The researcher found a statistic on a blog that says one out of every four teens will get an STD. Anyone can blog about pretty much anything. Many companies use blogs, too, so blogs can be commercial as well. The blogger here says he found the STD statistic at the American Social Health Association website. The researcher clicks the link and it takes him or her to that web page. While it is a useful statistic for an essay, the association doesn't say where the statistic comes from. Now what? The researcher can't cite the

It will likely be a long time before all worthwhile sources have been digitized and available online. Visiting a library to consult and copy content from secondary sources, and checking out the ones you can, will help fill in the gaps.

blogger because it's not his study or findings; he's merely reporting some-one else's information.

The researcher now has a decision to make. He or she can just simply cite the American Social Health Association website as the source. Or, the researcher can take the professional step of further confirming the fact by elsewhere. Option one is perfectly acceptable, but by taking the easier route, he or she is not going to have the strongest essay possible. Going

_ □ X

File   Edit   View   Favorites   Tools   Help

PERIODICALS ONLINE

Periodicals Online

We live in a world of media conglomerates. Many multinational corporations own dozens of smaller companies, or subsidiaries, and the diversity of owners seems to get smaller every year. Large broadcast companies own many smaller news and media operations. If the controlling company has certain political ideas, those ideas may filter to its news outlets. This means the news may be biased in favor of the company's agenda, especially in terms of ensuring its profits and reputation are maintained. For many big companies, news is really a thinly disguised form of marketing to push products, stars, or ideas. Interviews may be edited to portray subjects and stories in a certain light, and the onus is on the researcher to read between the lines, so to speak. In other words, what is really being said?

If your subject is a person, his or her quotes can be manipulated to make him or her appear a certain way. The savvy researcher tries to track down entire interviews rather than simply small parts, or excerpts. Seek full transcripts, if they are offered, or even audio or video interviews in their entirety via archived podcasts or videos on sites like YouTube or Vimeo. If there is no link to a full interview, it cannot hurt to contact the publication, whether an editor or the author of the article, to see if a copy can be obtained.

Newspapers, online and print, are a generally reliable source of factual coverage that, nonetheless, should still be substantiated via additional sources.

further will either confirm or refute this information. More is almost always better, within bounds.

The next step is to enter "one out of four teens will get an STD," or similar language, in a search engine. Pages of results reveal many links that confirm that one out of four teenage girls has an STD. High up in the results is a link to that information from the Centers for Disease Control and Prevention (CDC), an authority on disease in the United States. Clicking through may finally yield solid statistics on which the researcher can count. One result may be a press release in which the statistic, uncovered in a recent study, is featured prominently.

TEN GREAT QUESTIONS
to Ask a Research Librarian

1 Do you have any primary source book collections?

2 Do you provide access to any digital primary or secondary source collections?

3 Do you offer access to LexisNexis, Library Express, or other databases of archived articles, journals, and magazines?

4 Which of your digital periodical subscriptions offer entire articles for review?

5 What online electronic collections do you have access to here?

6 Do you have tutorials or classes on research and writing?

7 How do I access the library's online collection?

8 Do you have access to any notable digital university collections?

9 Where is information that is out of the ordinary for this topic found?

10 Can I print or download materials here directly?

Chapter 4

Ethics in Online Research

Much has changed those engaged in academic and business writing and projects since the advent of online research. Years ago, research was far more labor intensive and tedious. Often, information had to be physically tracked down in libraries, photocopied or hand copied, and cited by hand or by using a typewriter. Imagine doing all this work, including footnotes, bibliographies, supporting graphs, charts, and other data, before word processing software!

Supporting Materials—In Print

While increasingly rare, occasionally a teacher may request that a researcher save and provide print and hard copy sources. Or, the researcher will need to keep either excellent handwritten or typed notes. Researchers should maintain a go-to list of all sources, regardless of the manner in which the research was undertaken. Sources need to be numbered, as well as linked to the corresponding notes or photocopies. A hard copy report or presentation will have to be handed in with all of its supporting documentation.

Photocopying content might seem to be a thing of the past. Although it may be one day, there are still plenty of instances where you may need to make a physical copy of an article, image, or section of text.

Because the researcher will be using supporting information from these sources, he or she must take time to read and understand the material. Some resources cannot be checked out of the library, so it's important to "get" the material up front to be able to write about it later. It will also allow the researcher to highlight only important supporting facts rather than taking many pages of notes or photocopies. If more than one library or collection is used, the researcher should make a list of where the sources were obtained in the library.

With certain majors and fields of study, especially at the graduate school and doctoral levels, strict documentation is crucial. A master's thesis may be partially graded on the thoroughness of the researcher. Meanwhile, a doctoral defense (and a master's thesis defense, which is common in foreign universities) means defending one's findings before an academic committee—in other words, a group of professors.

Anything one includes in one's paper, including appendices, is fair game for the committee to grill the researcher about. So be prepared!

Nowadays, with electronic tools such as laptops, smartphones, and tablets, copying and pasting text is second nature. One can quickly copy and paste a URL, a paragraph of text, the source, and entire sections of material and drag and drop images into a report within seconds. Thousands of pages of research can be stored

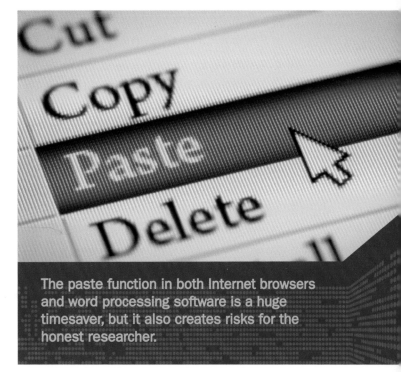

The paste function in both Internet browsers and word processing software is a huge timesaver, but it also creates risks for the honest researcher.

electronically, rather than toting around heavy piles of paper and giant academic tomes.

Ease enables speed, but also creates a huge potential for error. There are dangers associated with having it all at our fingertips. Researchers can easily forget where information comes from. Incredibly, some can even mistake someone else's work for their own. After becoming pros at tracking down real facts, researchers need to make sure they know how to keep their research straight in their heads, as well as in their files.

The Necessity of Citation

Everything and anything a researcher obtains from another source must be cited. Facts are useless unless they are linked to a source. Good citation and recordkeeping skills are things you can strengthen. For example, a teacher asks a student to write an essay on the rebuilding efforts in Louisiana after Hurricane Katrina. The White House's website states, "Significant progress has been made in the region." The researcher can cut and paste the quote from the web page into the essay. Simultaneously, the researcher must be in the habit of immediately copying the URL and date of the article into his or her list of sources. Always keep a separate document open where the information can be easily pasted. Numbering the facts that have been pasted into the essay also helps a great deal. Make sure to record as many details about the source as possible, including the date cited, the original date of the content, the author (or company or organization name, if there is no named author), and other necessary details, including the exact URL.

Now the researcher can get back to writing. He or she may write, for example, "According to the White House, 'significant progress has been made in the region.'" The researcher can also drop it next to his or her own words without mentioning the White House. If so, the researcher must use quotes. For example: "Changes are noticeable, and 'significant progress has been made in the region.'"[6] The source note "6" corresponds to the footnotes or the bibliography. That's where the source information that was copied and pasted earlier will be placed.

Teachers will always make sure that students know which form of citation is preferred. No matter what type is preferred, students must always keep the source details linked to the facts in some organizational way. It's truly annoying to have to leave out a useful fact after losing the trail of citation.

Researching Pitfalls

As the researcher navigates through multiple (perhaps even dozens of) online sources, he or she is learning about the topic. It may not seem important at first, but it is vital to keep track of what is already known versus new knowledge being gained through research.

A phrase might strike the researcher as memorable or compelling. You might take a second to figure out why you like it so much. Citation is especially important in such a case, lest the researcher later "misremember" that he or she didn't think of the pithy phrase him or herself. While it is often done on purpose, plagiarism, or copying someone else's work or ideas and passing them off as one's own, can happen just as easily by accident.

A researcher might like the way a website explains an idea. He or she innocently tries to recall it so it can be revisited or reworked later during writing. While typing away, the information just flows. The researcher might unknowingly repeat what was read earlier: someone else's work.

Sometimes, ideas or text just aren't coming and the researcher is desperate. He or she sees his or her own points expressed so well somewhere. "What's the problem with one little sentence from somewhere else?" he or she may rationalize. The researcher copies and pastes, and there it is—instant essay. It's not original text, though. Researchers beware: every teacher has read hundreds of essays. Teachers are often able to recognize in an instant writing that belongs to the student versus text lifted from elsewhere. One little copied sentence can—without a citation—turn any essay into a failure. The savvy researcher wants to avoid plagiarism at all costs.

Nowadays, the same technologies that allow you to find an exact phrase online in seconds can easily expose plagiarism, too. Many schools,

Former senator John Walsh of Montana (*right*), a career military man, pulled out of the 2014 election race to keep his seat after the U.S. Army War College revoked his master's degree; he was revealed to have plagiarized parts of a 2007 report.

universities, as well as individual instructors, have invested in plagiarism detection software. This software is used to find exact phrases across hundreds of thousands of sites and archived academic works, so beware if you intentionally (or even unintentionally) end up with another's words in your work without credit. The penalties for plagiarism can be academic censure (punishment) and even expulsion. It is also not worth it to risk one's future reputation for a shortcut.

THE DANGERS OF BIAS

File   Edit   View   Favorites   Tools   Help

The Dangers of Bias

Another danger for researchers is skewing the results of their research to support their personal opinions or advance their personal agendas. It is necessary to have point of view in a persuasive essay, and even in an objective academic report. Sometimes, one's opinion or analysis may not gel with the facts, especially as one delves further into one's research. It takes character to admit that you were wrong about something. The alternative is to fudge one's results. Scientific researchers have succumbed to this temptation in the past. For whatever reasons, they seek only the facts that will support their desired result. The same can happen as students gather their information. As with plagiarism, sometimes it is a conscious effort, while other times it is unconscious. Far from being a failure on your part, reporting results that contradict your original theory or personal opinion is a sign of good research and scholarship.

In addition, it is advisable to sit down and do some recreational reading on one's topic, engaging it as if one isn't writing a report, but reading for fun. Researchers should let ideas form in their minds around what is being read. This may inspire changes in the finished report. Great researchers don't stay stubbornly attached to the original essay idea. They simply change the essay and let the teacher know what happened. A teacher will probably tell his or her students that some of the greatest reports and presentations were led by the facts.

Good research practices will help you produce the kind of work you can be proud of and be confident in. Turning in your best effort will make giving a final presentation on your topic a breeze.

Remember always that no matter what your essay, report, or presentation is about, you are standing on the shoulders of the other researchers and writers who came before you. Asking permission to use media and citing research that you find online is not just done for the sake of following the rules but as a sign of respect. Well-researched academic works, especially when one reaches the halls of higher education, can live long past the class for which it is prepared. A teacher may keep a particularly good example for future students, and particularly stellar work might even be published in school publications or academic journals. The skills one gains by researching online the right way now are useful for a lifetime of intellectual inquiry and one's future career.

GLOSSARY

bias Unfair preference for one thing, or dislike of another.

browser An application that allows the user to surf the Internet.

censure Punishment for breaking a rule.

citation A quotation from a source.

cite To give credit to a source.

comparative essay An essay that compares two or more things.

controversial Provoking strong disagreement.

descriptive essay An essay that describes people, places, or things in a straightforward manner.

excerpt A passage or section taken from a larger whole.

HTML Hypertext markup language; code or instructions for Web-based applications.

infinite Limitless in size.

meta A prefix that means "beyond," "after," or "along with."

metasearch engine A website that searches search engines, compiling its results.

persuasive essay An essay that offers a factually supported opinion about a particular idea, theory, or opinion, written with the aim of persuading the reader to adopt a particular point of view.

plagiarism Copying someone else's work or idea and passing it off as your own.

primary sources Original documents, illustrations, photographs, artifacts, video, audio, and interviews that provide firsthand information about a topic.

search engine A system that searches the Web for information.

secondary sources Sources that interpret whatever primary sources are available.

substantiated Proven factually.

tertiary sources Sources where primary and secondary resources are collected.

transcript A complete written record of something.

URL Uniform resource locator, a specific address for online content.

validate To confirm or establish the truthfulness or accuracy of something.

American Library Association
50 East Huron
Chicago, IL 60611
(800) 545-2433
Website: http://www.ala.org
The American Library Association (ALA) strives to bring excellence and guidance to school librarians across the United States. The ALA's site offers KC (KidsConnect). This section has tips and tools to help you become more familiar and comfortable with the research process.

Library of Congress
101 Independence Avenue SE
Washington, DC 20540-1400
(202) 707-9779
Website: http://www.loc.gov
The Library of Congress serves as the research center for the U.S. Congress. Its website offers access to thousands of important primary source documents, images, and files. The Library of Congress is the largest library in the world.

National Archives and Records Administration
8601 Adelphi Road
College Park, MD 20740-6001
(866) 272-6272
Website: http://www.archives.gov
The National Archives and Records Administration's huge archive collects and manages important (and daily) documents created and used by the U.S. federal government.

Natural Resources Canada: The Atlas of Canada
615 Booth Street, Room 650
Ottawa, ON K1A 0E9
Canada
(613) 995-0947
(613) 996-4397 (hearing-impaired)
E-mail: info@atlas.gc.ca
Website: http://atlas.nrcan.gc.ca/site/english/index.html
Natural Resources Canada is Canada's official resource of maps and his-
    torical documents.

Statistics Canada Learning Resources
150 Tunney's Pasture Driveway
Ottawa, ON K1A 0T6
Canada
Website: http://www.statcan.ca/english/edu/students.htm
Statistics Canada Learning Resources is Canada's national statistics agency.
    It offers numerous resources for learning (and teaching) in school.

Websites

Because of the changing nature of Internet links, Rosen Publishing has developed an online list of websites related to the subject of this book. This site is updated regularly. Please use this link to access the list:

http://www.rosenlinks.com/DIL/Proj

FOR FURTHER READING

Bell, Suzanne S. *Librarian's Guide to Online Searching: Cultivating Database Skills for Research and Instruction*. 4th ed. Santa Barbara, CA: Libraries Unlimited, 2015.

Booth, Wayne C., Gregory G. Colomb, and Joseph M. Williams. *The Craft of Research* (Chicago Guides to Writing, Editing, and Publishing). 3rd ed. Chicago, IL: University of Chicago Press, 2008.

Gad, Victor. *The Research Virtuoso: How to Find Anything You Need to Know*. Toronto, Ontario: Annick Press, 2012.

Hock, Randolph. *The Extreme Searcher's Internet Handbook: A Guide for the Serious Searcher*. Medford, NJ: Information Today, Inc., 2013.

Lindeen, Mary. *Smart Online Searching: Doing Digital Research* (Searchlight Books: What Is Digital Citizenship?). Minneapolis, MN: Lerner Publishing, 2016.

Mann, Thomas. *The Oxford Guide to Library Research*. 4th ed. New York, NY: Oxford University Press, 2015.

Marcovitz, Hal. *Online Information and Research* (Issues in the Digital Age). San Diego, CA: Referencepoint Press, 2012.

Porterfield, Jason. *Conducting Basic and Advanced Searches* (Digital Information and Literacy). New York, NY: Rosen Publishing, 2011.

Randolph, Ryan. *New Research Techniques: Getting the Most Out of Search Engine Tools* (Digital and Information Literacy). New York, NY: Rosen Publishing, 2011.

Reinking, James A. *Strategies for Successful Writing: A Rhetoric, Research Guide, Reader and Handbook*. 10th ed. Upper Saddle River, NJ: Prentice Hall, 2014.

Sosulski, Kristen, and Ted Bongiovanni. *The Savvy Student's Guide to Online Learning*. New York, NY: Routledge Books, 2013.

BIBLIOGRAPHY

American Library Association. "Using Primary Sources." 2008. Retrieved August 5, 2015 (http://www.ala.org/rusa/sections/history/resources/pubs/usingprimarysources).

Gardiner, Eileen, and Ronald G. Musto. *The Digital Humanities: A Primer for Students and Scholars*. New York, NY: Cambridge University Press, 2015.

Gibaldi, Phyllis Franklin. *MLA Handbook for Writers of Research Papers*. 7th ed. New York, NY: Modern Language Association, 2009.

Mann, Thomas. *The Oxford Guide to Library Research*. 4th ed. New York, NY: Oxford University Press, 2015.

Netcraft Internet Services. "August 2008 Web Server Survey." Retrieved September 9, 2008 (http://news.netcraft.com/archives/Web_server_survey.html).

Public Broadcasting Systems. "Media Giants." 1995–2008. Retrieved September 5, 2008 (http://www.pbs.org/wgbh/pages/frontline/shows/cool/giants).

Quinn, Stephen, and Stephen Lamble. *Online Newsgathering: Research and Reporting for Journalism*. St. Louis, MO: Focal Press, 2007.

Schlein, Alan. *Find It Online: The Complete Guide to Online Research*. 4th ed. Tempe, AZ: Facts on Demand Press, 2014.

Turabian, Kate, Wayne C. Booth, and University of Chicago Press Staff. *A Manual for Writers of Research Papers, Theses, and Dissertations: Chicago Style for Students and Researchers*. Rev. ed. Chicago, IL: University of Chicago Press, 2011.

INDEX

About the Author

Pete Michalski is a writer who specializes in digital and computer technology and lives in Queens, NY.

Henrietta M. Lily is an award-winning children's author. She has worked as a fact-checker for print and digital organizations. She enjoys surfing, searching, and exploring the Web, both for information and for fun.

Photo Credits

Designer: Nicole Russo; Editor: Philip Wolny;
Photo Researcher: Philip Wolny